GW00891004

It's Easy To Play
Pops 8.

Wise Publications

London / New York / Paris / Sydney / Copenhagen / Madrid

Exclusive Distributors:

Music Sales Limited
8/9 Frith Street, London W1V 5TZ, England.

Music Sales Pty Limited
120 Rothschild Avenue, Rosebery, NSW 2018, Australia.

Order No. AM952480
ISBN 0-7119-7104-8

Music arranged by Stephen Duro.
Music processed by Allegro Reproductions.

Music Sales' complete catalogue describes thousands of titles and
is available in full colour sections by subject, direct from Music Sales Limited.
Please state your areas of interest and send a cheque/postal order for £1.50 for postage to:
Music Sales Limited, Newmarket Road, Bury St. Edmunds, Suffolk IP33 3YB.

Visit the Internet Music Shop at
http://www.musicsales.co.uk

Your Guarantee of Quality:
As publishers, we strive to produce every book to the highest commercial standards.
The music has been freshly engraved and the book has been carefully designed to minimise awkward page turns and to make playing from it a real pleasure.
Particular care has been given to specifying acid-free, neutral-sized paper made from pulps which have not been elemental chlorine bleached.
This pulp is from farmed sustainable forests and was produced with special regard for the environment.
Throughout, the printing and binding have been planned to ensure a sturdy, attractive publication which should give years of enjoyment.
If your copy fails to meet our high standards, please inform us and we will gladly replace it.

Printed in the United Kingdom by
Caligraving Limited, Thetford, Norfolk.

Barbie Girl

Words & Music by Soren Rasted, Claus Norreen, Rene Dif,
Lene Nystrom, Johnny Pederson & Karsten Delgado

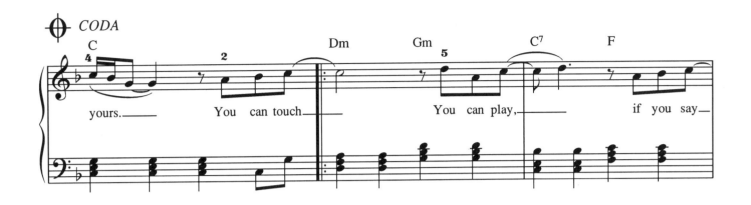

Falling Into You

Words & Music by Rick Nowles, Marie-Claire D'Ubalio & Billy Steinberg

you, this dream could come true and it feels so good fall-ing in-to you. I was a-fraid

to you. Fall-ing like a leaf, fall-ing like a star, find-ing a be-lief, fall-ing where you are. Catch me, don't let me drop!

fall - ing like— a star,

find - ing a

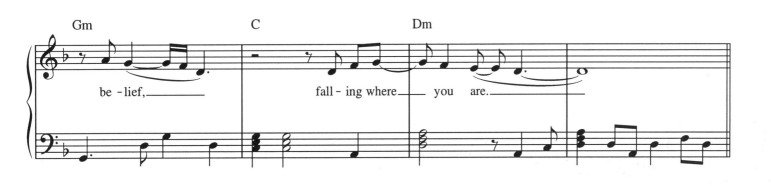

be - lief,

fall - ing where— you are.

Fall - ing in - to you,

fall - ing in - to you,

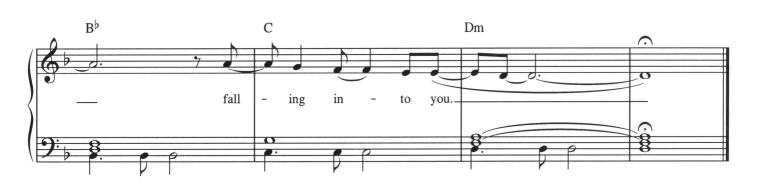

fall - ing in - to you.

I Believe I Can Fly

Words & Music by Robert Kelly

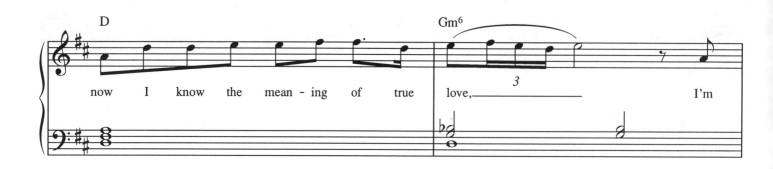

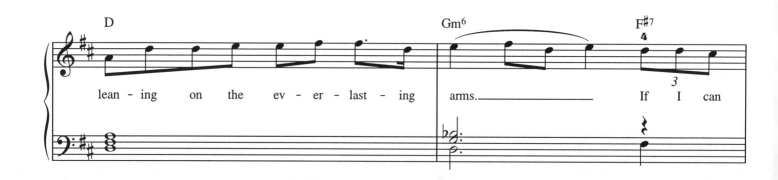

night and day,____ spread my wings and fly a-way,____ I be-lieve I can

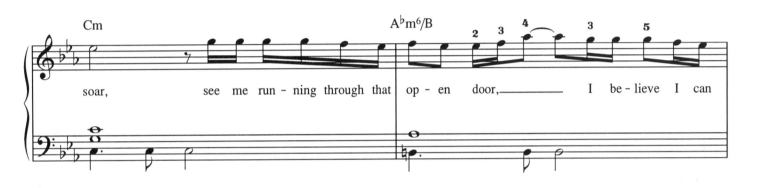

soar, see me run-ning through that op-en door,_____ I be-lieve I can

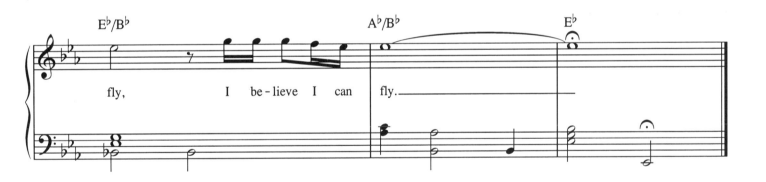

fly, I be-lieve I can fly.____

Verse 2:

See I was on the verge of breaking down,
Sometimes silence can seem so loud.
There are miracles in life I must achieve,
But first I know it stops inside of me.

Oh, if I can see it,
Then I can be it.
If I just believe it,
There's nothing to it.

As Long As You Love Me

Words & Music by Max Martin

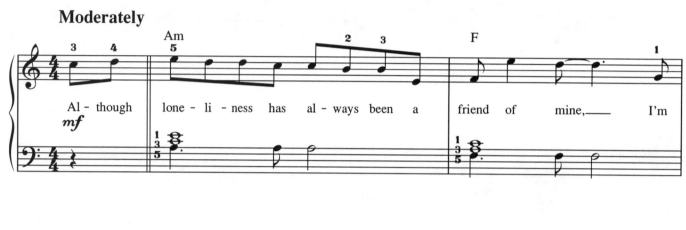

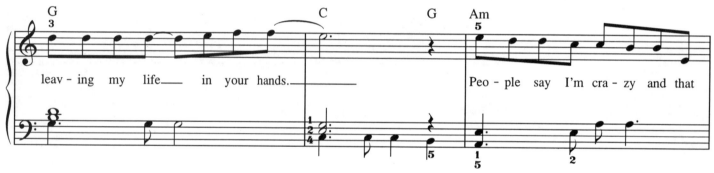

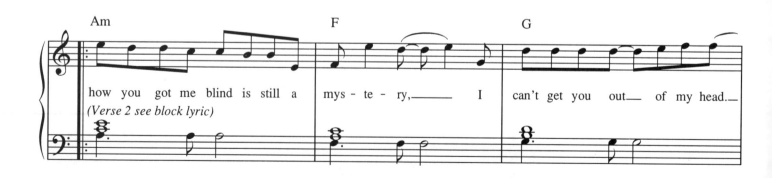

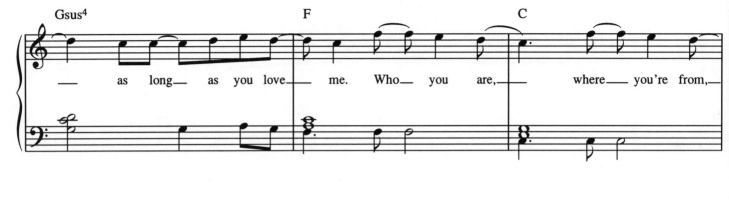

Verse 2:

Every little thing that you have said and done
Feels like it's deep within me
Doesn't really matter if you're on the run
It seems like we're meant to be.

I don't care *etc.*

Love Shine A Light

Words & Music by Kimberley Rew

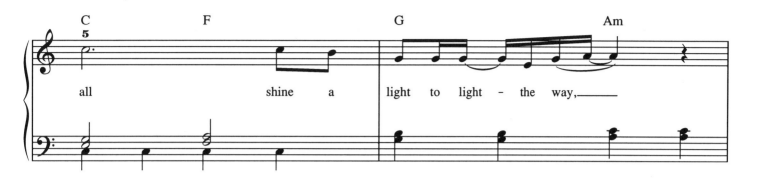

all   shine a   light to light - the way,_____

bro - thers and sis - ters__ in ev - 'ry lit - tle part, let our love__ shine a light in ev - 'ry

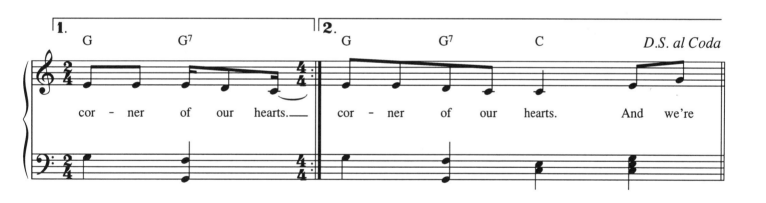

cor - ner of our hearts.__ cor - ner of our hearts. And we're

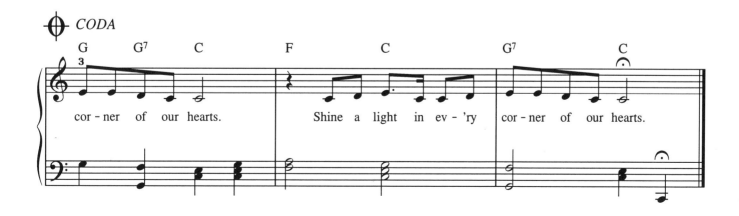

cor - ner of our hearts.   Shine a light in ev - 'ry   cor - ner of our hearts.

Power Of A Woman

Words & Music by Evan Rogers & Carl Sturken

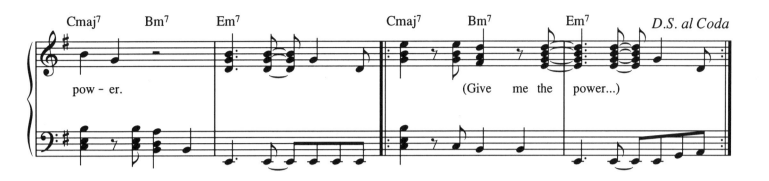

pow - er.

(Give me the power...)

D.S. al Coda

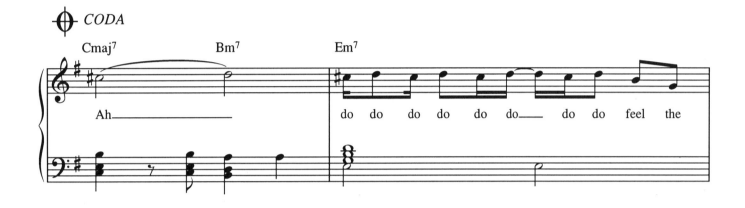

CODA

Ah_____

do do do do do do___ do do feel the

pow - er,

the pow - er.

Verse 2:

Please don't misunderstand
I need a strong man
Who'll be my soldier
Never give up the fight
I gotta know now
Baby let it show now
Can you keep the fire burning
Morning till night.

You're always caught up
In a one-way love affair
Livin' with your heart on the run
I've got the real thing
Come and get it if you dare
Let me tell you baby, don't you know I'm the one.

Rotterdam

Words & Music by Paul Heaton & David Rotheray

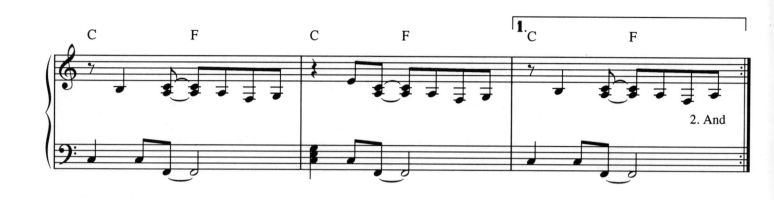

2. And

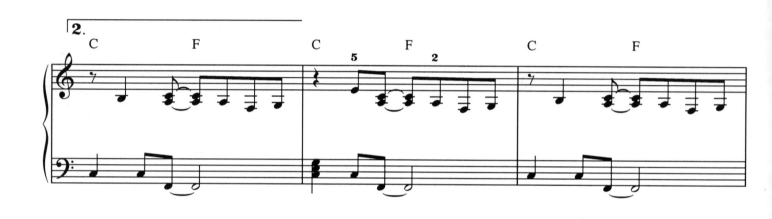

D.S. al Coda

The

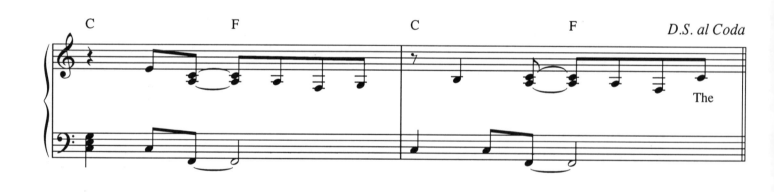

CODA

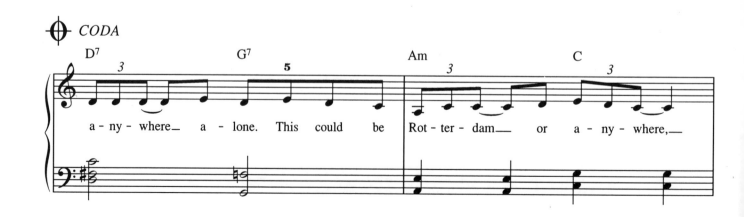

a - ny - where___ a - lone. This could be Rot - ter - dam___ or a - ny - where,___

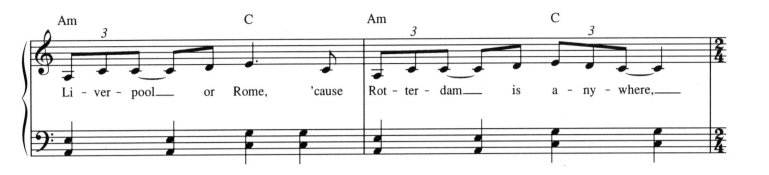

Li - ver - pool___ or Rome, 'cause Rot - ter - dam___ is a - ny - where,___

a - ny - where___ a lone, a - ny - where a - lone.___

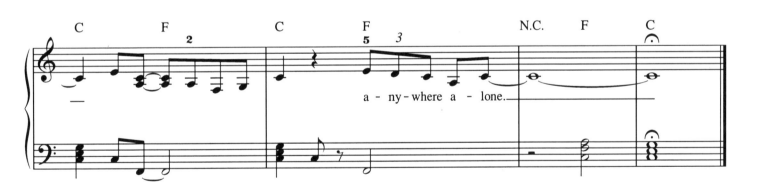

a - ny - where a - lone.

Verse 2:

And everyone is blonde
And everyone is beautiful.
And when blonde and beautiful are multiple
They become so dull and dutiful.
And when faced with dull and dutiful
They fire red warning flares,
Battle-khaki personality
With red underwear.

Spice Up Your Life

Words & Music by Geri Halliwell, Emma Bunton, Melanie Brown, Melanie Chisholm, Victoria Aadams, Richard Stannard & Matt Rowe

Slam it to the left (if you're hav-ing a good time), shake it to the right (if you know that you feel fine),

chi-cas to the front, uh___ uh, hi ci ya___ hold tight. hi ci ya___ hold tight.

Spoken: Fla -

men - co, lam - ba - da, but hip - hop is hard - er, we moon - walk the fox - trot then

pol - ka the sal - sa. Shake it shake it shake it, ha - ka.

Shake it shake it shake it, ha - ka.

Stand By Me

Words & Music by Noel Gallagher

Moderately

Em

A⁷

don't you know___ the
cold and wind and rain don't know___ they

C

D

1.

on - ly seem to come and go a - way.___

2.

G

D

5 4 3

Stand by___ me,___
no - bo - dy knows___

Am⁷
2 1
5
3

the way it's gon - na be.

C F D⁷ G

Stand by___ me,___

D

Am⁷

C F D⁷

no - bo - dy knows___
the way it's gon - na be.

37

Verse 2:

Times are hard when things have got no meaning
I've found a key upon the floor
Maybe you and I will not believe in
The things we find behind the door.

So what's the matter *etc.*

Verse 3:

If you're leaving will you take me with you
I'm tired of talking on my phone
There is one thing I can never give you
My heart will never be your home.

So what's the matter *etc.*

The Day We Find Love

Words & Music by Eliot Kennedy & Helen Boulding

on - ly thing I'm ask - ing_____ 'cause I need you to re - mem - ber me_____

_____ as the on - ly one___ who set___ you free,_____

may - be time a - lone___ will make___ you see___

___ how deep___ our love___ could___ be,_____ you know it's

nev - er too late._____ 'Cause I know___

this is-n't the first___ time, won't be the last___ time. I sur-ren-

-der my soul___ 'cause you're al-ways keep-ing me wait - ing, an-ti-ci-pa-

-ting,___ the day___ we find love___ once a-gain.___

Re - mem - ber me___

as the on - ly one who set___ you free,___

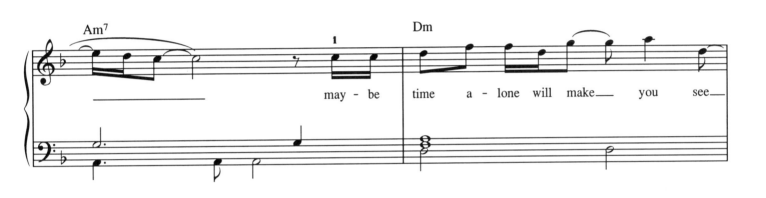

may - be time a - lone will make___ you see___

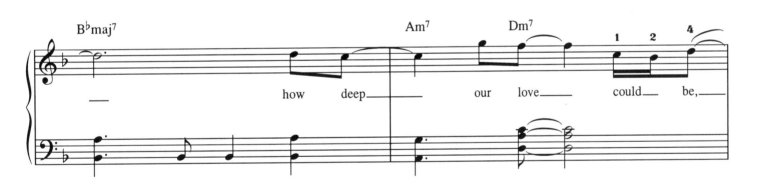

how deep___ our love___ could___ be,

no it's nev - er too late.___ 'Cause I know___

this is - n't the first — time, won't be the last — time. I sur - ren -

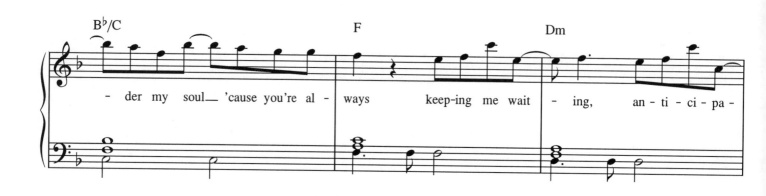

- der my soul — 'cause you're al - ways keep-ing me wait - ing, an - ti - ci - pa -

- ting, — the day — we find love — once a - gain. —

Verse 2:

I won't give up while there's a glimmer of a chance,
A dream that's never-ending, inviting love and a perfect romance.
A burning passion, oh baby, you're my destiny,
But the message I'm receiving is you're through with me but I'll be there,
Even though you tell me you don't care.
How could you forget the times we've shared?
Don't throw our love away,
You know it's never too late.

You Must Love Me

Music by Andrew Lloyd Webber
Lyrics by Tim Rice

Moderately

how do we keep___ all our pas - sions a - live as

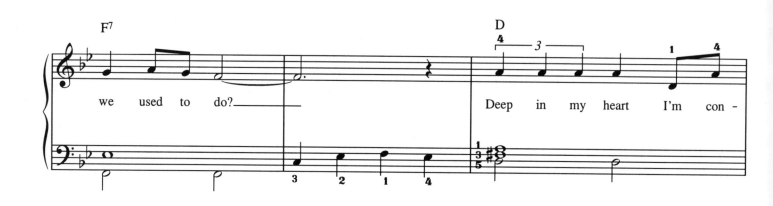

we used to do?___ Deep in my heart I'm con -

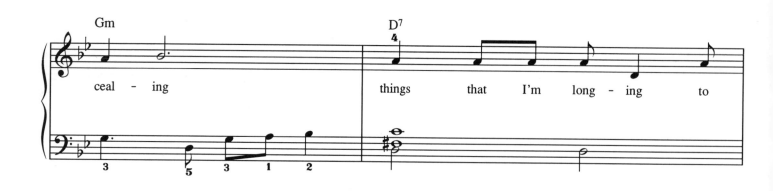

ceal - ing things that I'm long - ing to

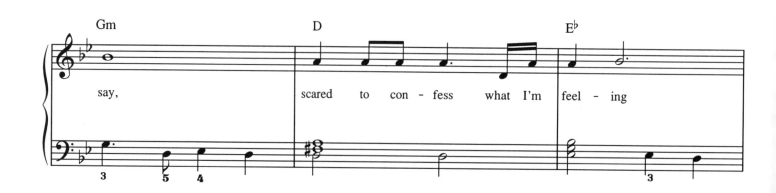

say, scared to con - fess what I'm feel - ing

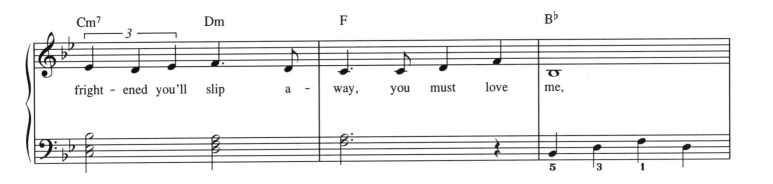

fright - ened you'll slip   a - way,   you must love   me,

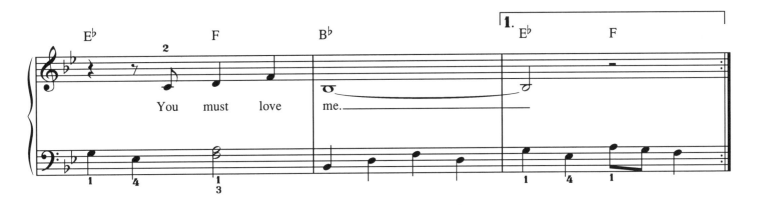

You   must   love   me. ___

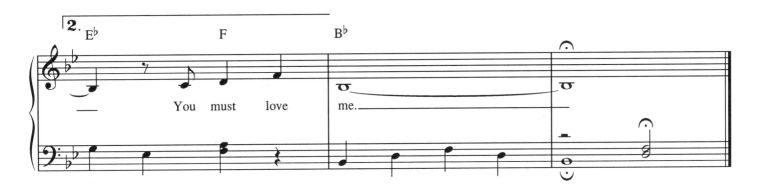

___   You   must   love   me. ___

Verse 2: (Instrumental 8 bars)

Why are you at my side?
How can I be any use to you now?
Give me a chance and I'll let you see how
Nothing has changed.
Deep in my heart I'm concealing
Things that I'm longing to say,
Scared to confess what I'm feeling
Frightened you'll slip away,
You must love me.

The Beatles

Enya

Phil Collins

Van Morrison

Bob Dylan

Sting

Paul Simon

Tracy Chapman

Eric Clapton

Pink Floyd

New Kids On The Block

Bryan Adams

Tina Turner

Elton John

Bee Gees

Whitney Houston

AC/DC

Bringing you the words

All the latest in rock and pop. Plus the brightest and best in West End show scores. Music books for every instrument under the sun. And exciting new teach-yourself ideas like "Let's Play Keyboard" - in cassette/book packs, or on video. Available from all good music shops.

and music

Music Sales' complete catalogue lists thousands of titles and is available free from your local music shop, or direct from Music Sales Limited. Please send a cheque or postal order for £1.50 (for postage) to:

Music Sales Limited
Newmarket Road,
Bury St Edmunds,
Suffolk IP33 3YB

Buddy

Five Guys Named Moe

Les Misérables

West Side Story

Phantom Of The Opera

Show Boat

The Rocky Horror Show

Bringing you the world's best music.